# The Story of Washington, DC

Curtis Slepian, M.A.

## Consultants

**Brian Allman**
*Principal*
Upshur County Schools, West Virginia

**James D. Zimmer Jr., M.A., M.S.Ed.**
*Instructional Coordinator for Social Studies*
Cecil County Public Schools, Maryland

## Publishing Credits

Rachelle Cracchiolo, M.S.Ed., *Publisher*
Emily R. Smith, M.A.Ed., *SVP of Content Development*
Véronique Bos, *VP of Creative*
Dona Herweck Rice, *Senior Content Manager*
Dani Neiley, *Editor*
Fabiola Sepulveda, *Series Graphic Designer*

**Image Credits:** p5 Shutterstock/Sean Pavone; p6 Library of Congress [73694572]; p7 (top) British Museum, London; p7 (bottom) Gerald R. Ford Presidential Library and Museum/NARA; p8 Library of Congress [74692109]; p9 (top) Library of Congress [LC-DIG-ppmsca-30579]; p10 (bottom) Library of Congress [LC-DIG-ppmsca-23076]; p11 (top) Library of Congress [2104-2104001]; p11 (bottom) Alamy Stock Photo/North Wind Picture Archives; p12 National Capital Planning Commission, Washington, DC.; p13 (top) Library of Congress [LC-DIG-hec-03446]; p14 Library of Congress [LC-DIG-ppmsca-53534]; p16 (top) Bridgeman Images; p16 (bottom) Library of Congress [LC-DIG-ppmsca-24360]; p17 Getty Images/CNP; p18 Library of Congress [LC-USZ62-2574]; p19 Library of Congress [LC-DIG-hec-26800]; p20 (bottom) Getty Images/The Washington Post; p25 (top) Shutterstock/Cvandyke; p25 (bottom) Library of Congress [LC-DIG-ppmsca-19405]; p26 (top) District of Columbia DMV; p27 Library of Congress [LC-USZC4-3623]; p32 Shutterstock/Joseph Sohm; all other images from iStock and/or Shutterstock

## Library of Congress Cataloging-in-Publication Data

Names: Slepian, Curtis, author.
Title: The story of Washington, D.C. / Curtis Slepian, M.A.
Description: Huntington Beach : Teacher Created Materials, [2022] | Includes index. | Audience: Grades 4-6 | Summary: "Washington, DC, is more than just the U.S. capital. It plays a big role in the nation's history. This book tells the story of DC from the beginning. It tells about all the people and events that make it what it is today. You will see how DC grew from swamp land into an amazing international city with countless attractions to teach its visitors about the nation's past and present"-- Provided by publisher.
Identifiers: LCCN 2022021229 (print) | LCCN 2022021230 (ebook) | ISBN 9781087691015 (paperback) | ISBN 9781087691176 (ebook)
Subjects: LCSH: Washington (D.C.)--History--Juvenile literature.
Classification: LCC F194.3 .S496 2022 (print) | LCC F194.3 (ebook) | DDC 975.3--dc23/eng/20220506
LC record available at https://lccn.loc.gov/2022021229
LC ebook record available at https://lccn.loc.gov/2022021230

**Shown on the cover is the Washington Monument in Washington, DC.**

**TCM** Teacher Created Materials

5482 Argosy Avenue
Huntington Beach, CA 92649
www.tcmpub.com

**ISBN 978-1-0876-9101-5**
© 2023 Teacher Created Materials, Inc.

# Table of Contents

# Discovering Washington, DC

You are standing in front of the Washington Monument. You have seen many pictures of it. In person, it's even more awesome! You turn around. In the distance is the **Capitol** building. The giant white dome is amazing in real life. Washington, DC, is full of cool sights like this. Everywhere you look are statues and monuments and huge marble buildings. But the city is special for another big reason. Washington, DC, is the capital of the United States. It is the seat of America's government. Decisions are made here that can change the lives of all Americans.

Jefferson Memorial

National Mall

Library of Congress

Washington, DC, has helped shape the nation like no other city has. The most important government activities happen here. The country's laws are made in the Capitol building. The U.S. Supreme Court is the top court in the land. The White House is home to the U.S. president and their family.

DC is also like a catalog for the nation's history. Here, America's past is saved in places such as the National Archives, the Library of **Congress**, and many museums. Even its neighborhoods have a rich history. The city is packed with symbols of America's power and importance.

## Tall Order

Washington has no skyscrapers. Some people think there is a law that says that buildings cannot be higher than the Washington Monument (554 feet, 7 inches; 169 meters). Not true. The law says no building can be taller than 130 feet (40 meters) except in a few small areas. This allows the streets to get plenty of sunlight.

# The Early Years

European Americans have lived in Washington, DC, for hundreds of years. But American Indians lived on that land for thousands of years before that. Present-day DC sits near the Anacostia and Potomac Rivers. Early American Indians found this to be a great place to live. The rivers gave them plenty of fish. Nearby forests were full of animals to hunt. The people grew beans, potatoes, and other vegetables. They used stone to make tools and bowls.

By the 1600s, the region's largest tribe was the **Nacotchtank** peoples. They built villages in the area. One village was where the Capitol now stands. They grew vegetables on land where the Library of Congress and Supreme Court buildings now sit. The Nacotchtank peoples traded with other peoples along the East Coast.

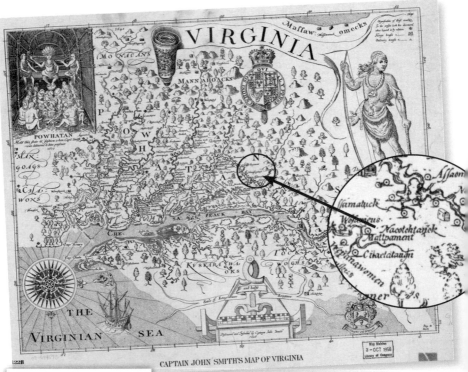

John Smith's 1612 map

But their lives changed in 1607. That was when the first Europeans arrived in the region. The explorers were led by an Englishman named John Smith. Over time, the English took over much of the Nacotchtank land. Forty years after the English showed up, only 25 percent of the native people were left. Disease and war had killed many of them. By the late 1600s, the Nacotchtank peoples were almost gone. Their land became part of the colonies. The few remaining members of the tribe folded into the Piscataway tribe, which exists to this day.

Secoton village painted by John White, 1585

## First Residents

Presidents were not the first people to live on White House land. In 1975, a swimming pool was dug on the White House South Lawn. Experts found pottery and other human-made objects in the soil. They were made by American Indians who lived there long before Europeans did. In this photo, President Gerald Ford and others look at the excavation.

# A Capital Idea

Washington, DC, was not the first U.S. capital. It was not even the second or third. But it was the final one. The U.S. **Constitution** was signed in 1787. It said the U.S. government would be in charge of creating a new capital. This capital could not be more than 10 miles (16 kilometers) square. But where to build it?

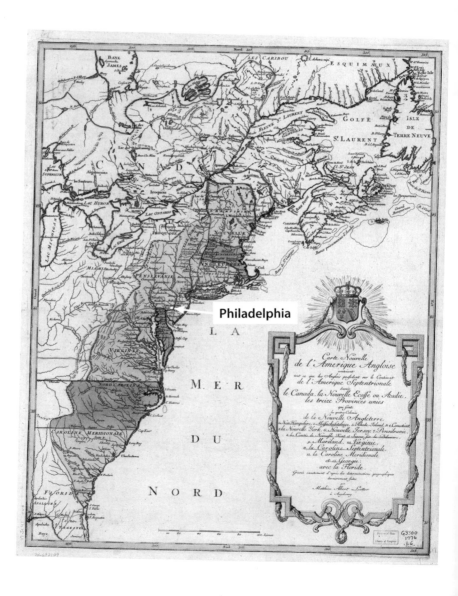
Philadelphia

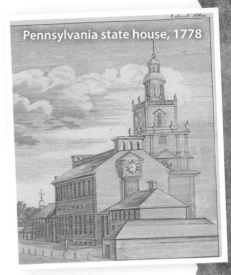
Pennsylvania state house, 1778

Northerners wanted it in the North. Southerners pushed for the South. New Yorker Alexander Hamilton and Virginian Thomas Jefferson made a deal. Hamilton wanted to get an important law passed in Congress. Jefferson would help pass it. But he would only help if the South got its way. Hamilton gave the thumbs-up. Philadelphia would be the U.S. capital from 1790 until 1800. Then, the capital would move south near the Potomac River.

Maryland and Virginia gave up some land to form the city. President George Washington thought it was the perfect spot. One reason was that the site was about halfway up the East Coast. It was close to both northern and southern states. And the president hoped it would be the "gateway to the interior." The new capital might connect the western part of the country to the eastern.

The capital was named for—who else?—George Washington. The area around the city was called the **District** of Columbia. The name honored Christopher Columbus, who was thought to be the founder of the land for the settlers from Europe.

## The Great Eight

Carpenters' Hall, Philadelphia

Washington, DC, was the ninth U.S. capital. The first U.S. government, the Continental Congress, moved around a lot. Wherever it met became the capital. The first eight capitals were Baltimore, York, Lancaster, Philadelphia, Princeton, Trenton, Annapolis, and New York City.

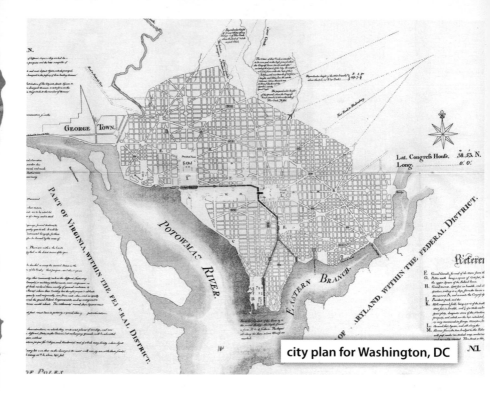

city plan for Washington, DC

# A City Grows

George Washington wanted the capital to be a grand city. He hired Pierre Charles L'Enfant to plan it. The **engineer** came up with a design of long avenues and majestic squares. But government leaders turned down his plan. So, in 1800, when DC became the nation's capital, it was not close to grand! There were few houses, and the streets were dirt paths. The White House (which used to be called the Executive Mansion) and the Capitol building were not finished. Then, the British burned both buildings during the War of 1812.

U.S. Capitol after it was burned

But Washington, DC, slowly recovered and grew. The Capitol and White House were rebuilt. In the 1830s, the first railroad line reached DC. Trains brought people curious to see the capital. The population increased during the Civil War. Thousands of soldiers arrived to protect the city. Washington, DC, also became filled with wounded soldiers. Others came to care for them. The population of the city continued to grow.

construction of the U.S. Capitol

But after the war, many people returned home. They left behind a city of run-down buildings and failed businesses. Congress would not spend money on the capital. But in 1871, it let the city rule itself for a few years. Leaders built new schools and markets. Streets were paved. There was a feeling that the city could one day be as grand as once imagined.

## For Good Measure

Benjamin Banneker was an African American who assisted in the layout of Washington, DC. He worked with the main **surveyor** of the new capital. Banneker helped create the boundaries of Washington, DC. He used a telescope to get exact measurements.

## Ups and Downs

In 1900, Washington, DC, had a birthday. It was 100 years old. Now, public officials wanted to make the city beautiful. They dusted off L'Enfant's plans and agreed to new buildings that were made to look like ancient Greek and Roman temples. Concert halls and museums opened. Fancy stores sprang up. Magnificent foreign **embassies** lined several avenues. The city was a magnet for the rich. They lived in **mansions** in neighborhoods, such as Dupont Circle. But the city was also home to many poor people. They lived in dark, dirty streets called **alleys**. They were out of sight of the rich.

In 1929, America was brought low by the **Great Depression**. Millions of people were out of work. A few years later, President Franklin Roosevelt had a solution to end the hard times. He created government jobs. Thousands of people came to DC to fill them. Some people worked on big public projects. They helped finish the Supreme Court building and the Library of Congress.

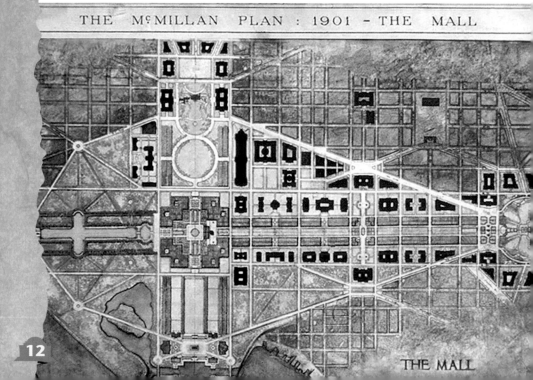

THE McMILLAN PLAN : 1901 - THE MALL

THE MALL

## Lincoln's Memorial

The Lincoln **Memorial** almost did not happen. It was thought the site for it was too swampy. But the swamp was drained, and the memorial was finished in 1922.

Then, another event shook the nation. In 1941, the United States entered World War II. Washington, DC, became a big part of the war effort. New workers and soldiers crowded the city. Many of the people who arrived were women who wanted to help the country in any way they could.

The war ended in 1945. America had helped defeat its enemies. Now, DC was a worldwide symbol for democracy.

**National Mall in Washington, DC**

# The Comeback Capital

By the 1950s, the United States had grown into a dominating world leader. And Washington, DC, was among the most influential capitals on Earth. Yet more and more locals were leaving the city. They were moving to **suburbs** in Virginia and Maryland. Families wanted more space and lower taxes. A few people packed their bags because they feared Russia might drop an atomic bomb on DC. Some Washington, DC, agencies, such as the CIA, moved their headquarters out of the city.

Even more people fled in the 1960s. Some hated the noisy protests against the Vietnam War. Others were upset when a riot took place in 1968. Some areas of the city were burned down. Crime was a major problem in the city. Things were so bad that Congress stepped in. It passed tough anti-crime laws.

But things began to get better. What turned it around? A lot of it had to do with something under the ground. In the 1970s, Washington, DC, leaders built a **subway** system. Now, it was easier to get around town. Riders could explore new neighborhoods. Nice apartment houses went up near subway stops. Young people started to move back to DC. The city was much safer than it had been.

effects from the 1968 Shaw riots

## Track Record

The Washington, DC, subway is called the Metro. It is
one of the busiest U.S. subway systems. In one year,
about 174 million people ride it. The most people who
rode it in one day was in 2009. This was the day Barack
Obama was sworn in as president.

1913 march for women's right to vote

## The Power of Protest

The U.S. Constitution protects the right to assemble peacefully. And one of America's favorite places to assemble is Washington, DC. Protestors there can catch the ears of lawmakers.

Over the years, there have been marches for and against many causes. A protest took place in 1913 when women marched for their right to vote. In the 1960s and 1970s, people often protested the Vietnam War. Earlier, in 1932, many angry World War I soldiers came to Washington. They said the government owed them money. Their protest did not work, but their cause made world headlines. The lesson? What happens in DC does not stay just in DC! It gets everyone's attention.

Vietnam War protest

Washington, DC, has been the scene of many **civil rights** protests. In 1957, there was a march for voting rights. Martin Luther King Jr. said, "Give us the ballot." Later, people marched to end school **segregation**. Perhaps the most famous demonstration took place in 1963. It was called the March on Washington for Jobs and Freedom. That is when Dr. King made his "I Have a Dream" speech. Recently, the Black Lives Matter movement demonstrated throughout DC. It seems DC is still *the* place to get your views heard.

Martin Luther King Jr. speaks at the March on Washington.

## Marching Millions

The largest single-day march in U.S. history took place in 2017. It was part of the Women's March on Washington. About 500,000 people attended the DC rally for women's rights and other causes. It is believed that more than 4.5 million people marched in support throughout the United States on that day. About 7 million people joined in around the world!

# A Challenging Path to Success

African Americans have played a major role in the capital's history. Slavery has as well. Washington, DC, was formed from land taken from Maryland and Virginia. About half of all enslaved people in the country lived in those states. So, Black people made up a quarter of the city's population in 1800. Some white visitors saw enslaved people in chains for the first time while there. They were shocked! Wasn't this the capital of democracy?

By 1830, the city's Black population was made up of about half free and half enslaved people. Some local people worked against slavery. Their voices helped bring an end to slavery in DC in 1862. During the Civil War, many African Americans came to the city. They wanted to fight for the Union. Most of them were freed people. Others had escaped from slavery.

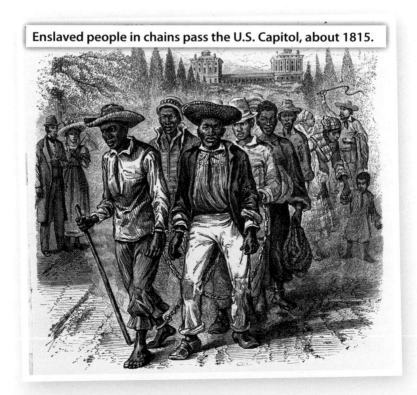

Enslaved people in chains pass the U.S. Capitol, about 1815.

Workers strike in Washington, DC.

By 1900, Washington, DC, had the largest percentage of Black people of any U.S. city. Over the years, they made their own communities. They ran their own stores. They went to their own schools. Black scholars and thinkers came to DC. But racism was still a way of life there. So, Black people took action in the 1930s and 1940s. They did not shop in racist stores. They held **sit-ins** in segregated restaurants.

One big issue was that the U.S. government would not hire Black workers. African Americans threatened to protest in the capital. The government backed down and changed its policy.

## Class Act

DC's Howard University was founded in 1867. It was mainly for African American students. At that time, most schools would not accept Black students. Today, Howard University is a top U.S. school. Some famous graduates are U.S. Supreme Court Justice Thurgood Marshall, Vice President Kamala Harris, and actor Chadwick Boseman.

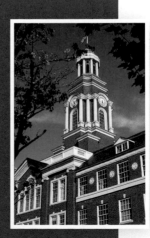

historic houses in the Shaw neighborhood

## On the Rise

In the 1950s, the civil rights movement grew. The United States passed laws to try to end racial injustice. This mattered to people in Washington, DC. Black Americans were now half the city's population. In the 1960s, peaceful protests against racism took place in the city. But in 1968, Black leader and activist Martin Luther King Jr. was killed in Memphis, Tennessee. His death touched off riots in the Shaw neighborhood. It had been a center of the city's Black life. The riots destroyed many stores and public areas. As a result, many white people began to leave the city. By 1975, nearly three-fourths of the population in the capital was Black. Then, Black families started to leave, too.

mural of singer Marvin Gaye in Washington, DC

But this was not the end of Shaw and DC. In time, people returned. They brought back a vibrant culture and community. People now enjoy Shaw's theaters, bookstores, and places to eat. Artists in Shaw and other neighborhoods have drawn street murals of great African Americans. Black history is marked throughout the city. You can check out the house Frederick Douglass once lived in. Douglass was once an enslaved person. He worked to end slavery. The Martin Luther King Jr. Memorial moves people, just as the man himself did. The National Museum of African American History and Culture tells the long story of Black people in America. It shows how they have helped build the nation.

## The Fighting 54th

The Shaw neighborhood was named for Robert Gould Shaw. He was a white Civil War officer who led the African American Massachusetts 54th **regiment**. Many of those troops died bravely in battle. One of these soldiers was the first African American to win the Medal of Honor.

Chesapeake and Ohio Canal National Historical Park in Georgetown, Washington, DC

# A Walk through History

Washington, DC, has loads of historic neighborhoods. The oldest is now known as Georgetown. In 1751, it was an English town named for King George II. In 1871, it became part of DC. Want to take a trip back in time? Walk along Georgetown's **cobblestone** streets. They are lined with old wooden houses and mansions. Or hike along the Chesapeake and Ohio Canal. This stretch of water was formed in 1828. The Foggy Bottom neighborhood has a funny name. Why? It was often covered in fog and smoke from factories. *Bottom* means it is a low-lying area.

Foggy Bottom has a famous address as well: 1600 Pennsylvania Avenue. That is the address of the White House. John Adams was the first president to live in it. Every president since then has called it home. Many of them made changes to the building. Now, the First Family enjoys a home and workspace with 132 rooms and 35 bathrooms! But they do not live there alone. The White House is home to hundreds of workers, guests, and more.

Two-thirds of the U.S. government is in the Capitol Hill neighborhood. Its highest point is the Capitol building. It is 288 feet (88 meters) tall. Here, Congress debates and makes laws. Nearby is the U.S. Supreme Court building. Inside, lawyers argue important cases before the justices. Close by is also the Library of Congress, the largest library in the world. It holds 170 million books and other objects.

## Play Ball!

A baseball diamond used to be a ball's throw from the White House. The first baseball clubs in Washington, DC, played on that field in 1860. President Andrew Johnson watched games there, and President Ulysses Grant even umpired games.

National Mall

## The Marvelous Mall

The National Mall stretches from the Capitol to the Potomac River. On the Mall between the Capitol and the Washington Monument is a long, green field. People play athletic games there. They hold protests. They watch Fourth of July fireworks. The Mall is called "America's Front Yard." But it was not always a fun place to hang out. It was once a marsh. Cattle grazed on it. Later, a railroad station was built on it. Today, the Mall is surrounded by monuments and memorials. It is also surrounded by museums and art galleries. And they are all free to visit!

Lincoln Memorial

The Mall is the city's most popular place to visit. One of its top attractions is the National Museum of American History. It has Abraham Lincoln's hat, Kermit the Frog, pieces of Plymouth Rock, and other objects from the nation's past. The National Air and Space Museum holds nearly everything that flies, from the Wright

National Museum of the American Indian

Brothers' plane to a *Mercury* capsule. The National Museum of the American Indian exhibits the culture and lives of native peoples. A mile from the Capitol is the Washington Monument. Climb its 897 steps to the top, if you can! Farther on is the Lincoln Memorial. From there, it is a short walk to the Vietnam Veterans Memorial and the Korean War Veterans Memorial. One trip to the Mall can teach a lot about America!

## Song of Freedom

Marian Anderson was a famous African American opera singer. In 1939, she was supposed to give a concert at Washington's Constitution Hall. But the hall's owners would not let her perform because of her race. So, Anderson sang on the steps of the Lincoln Memorial before 75,000 people.

# The 51st State?

"End taxation without **representation**." That slogan is written on many Washington, DC, license plates. The people who live there pay taxes to the U.S. government just like everyone else. But they have no senators. They have only one representative in Congress. But that person cannot vote. People in DC were not allowed to vote for a U.S. president until 1961. They could not even vote for a mayor until 1974.

Why is DC treated this way? This is how it is written into the Constitution. It says that the capital is to be controlled by the U.S. government. Congress makes the decisions about the district, including how to vote.

Washington, DC

Washington, DC, is a city. If it were a state, it would not be controlled by Congress. Should Washington, DC, be the 51st state? Some people say no. That would go against the Constitution. They fear it would have more power over the U.S. government than other states because of the work that is done there. But some people say yes. More people live in the city than in the states of Wyoming and Vermont. Those states have senators. Each has a representative who votes in Congress. Why shouldn't Washington, DC? They believe the people of the city should control their own lives.

City or state, Washington, DC, will always have great influence on American life. It will always be a place to understand America's past and present and its hopes for the future.

## Name Changer

If Washington became a state, it would get a new name. One of the names proposed for DC as a state is New Columbus. Another is State of Washington, Douglass Commonwealth. This name honors Frederick Douglass, who lived in the city for many years.

# Map It!

Washington, DC, is a city full of great things to see. Many maps of the area show the locations of these sights. But you can make your own map of DC's top attractions. Choose one of the following ideas:

1. Draw the outline of Washington, DC. On your map, place a symbol and name for each attraction you want to check out in person.

2. Draw the outline of Washington, DC. Add more sights that you wish existed in the city. Show memorials or monuments of people or groups from the past or the present. Name a museum for any subject you wish. Name new parks, and place them on your map.

3. Create a puzzle map. First, draw the outline of the National Mall. Place symbols of buildings, memorials, and monuments where they appear on the Mall. Number each symbol. Below the map, write the numbers. Next to each number, write one sentence that describes the place without naming it. See if others can determine the name of the sights based on the clues and the locations on the map.

Smithsonian Institution Building, also called The Castle

White House

Smithsonian National Air and Space Museum

Smithsonian Museum of Natural History

# Glossary

**alleys**—narrow streets between two buildings

**Capitol**—the building where the U.S. Congress meets

**civil rights**—the rights of personal liberty each U.S. citizen should have

**cobblestone**—a round stone used to pave streets or sidewalks

**Congress**—the U.S. Senate and House of Representatives

**Constitution**—the document that describes the laws and the system of government of the United States

**district**—an area created for a government's business

**embassies**—buildings where people work to represent foreign countries

**engineer**—a person who designs and builds complicated objects or systems

**Great Depression**—a time in the 1930s when the United States' and world economies were bad

**mansions**—very large houses

**memorial**—an object that honors a person or people who are no longer alive

**Nacotchtank**—an American Indian tribe who lived on the land that would become Washington, DC

**regiment**—a military unit made up of many soldiers

**representation**—the act of speaking or acting for a person or group of people so they can be represented in a legislative body

**segregation**—separating people because of their race or other reasons

**sit-ins**—protests where people refuse to leave places of business that practice discrimination

**suburbs**—small towns near bigger cities

**subway**—a system of underground trains in a city

**surveyor**—a person who measures an area of land

# Index

# Learn More!

Frederick Douglass led an amazing life. He was born an enslaved person in 1818. In 1838, he escaped to the North. There, he spoke out against slavery and talked about it with President Abraham Lincoln. He wrote three books about his life and wrote and gave speeches about racism. Douglass moved to Washington, DC, in 1872. It is said that he was the most photographed American in the 1800s.

✳ Find out more about Frederick Douglass.

✳ Imagine you are Douglass and that he kept a journal.

✳ Choose three big events from his life. For each event, write an entry in his journal. Describe his experiences as if you were him.

Frederick Douglass National Historic Site

# Read and Respond

1. Land from which two states was combined to form Washington, DC?

2. Why did the population of Washington, DC, get larger during the Civil War?

3. Why is DC a common place to stage a protest march or demonstration?

4. What are some reasons why Washington, DC, is an excellent place to learn about American history?

5. Which locations would you like to visit in Washington, DC?  Why?

6. How did Washington, DC, play a part in the civil rights movement?

# The Story of Washington, DC

Washington, DC, is more than just the U.S. capital. It plays a big role in the nation's history. This book tells the story of DC from the beginning. It tells about all the people and events that make it what it is today. You will see how DC grew from swamp land into an amazing international city with countless attractions to teach its visitors about the nation's past and present.

921602

**Reading Levels**
Lexile®: 670L
Guided Reading: U

**TCM** | Teacher Created Materials

ISBN-13: 978-1-0876-9101-5

90000

9 781087 691015